Legislative Essentials for Glamping Accommodation Lodgings Guide

This work Copyright ©Rob Farrow, 2018

All rights Reserved.

Rob Farrow reserves the right to be identified as the moral author of this work. No part of this work may be reproduced, stored in a retrieval system, or transmitted in any form or by any means – without the prior consent of the publisher.

Cover Photography Copyright ©Rob Farrow, 2018
Edited by Katriona E MacMillan

Legislative Essentials for Glamping Accommodation Lodgings Guide
Rob Farrow

Table of Contents

Introduction 5
Foreword 7
Before you start 9
    Planning 9
    Site Licence 10
    Fire Safety 10
    Building Regulations 11
    Water 11
    Rubbish 12
    Design 12
    Signage 12
    First Aid 13
Insurance 14
    Employers Liability Insurance 14
    Public Liability Insurance 14
    Appropriate and Adequate Insurance Cover 15
Marketing 16
    Social Media 16
Bookings 17
    Taking Bookings 17
    Honouring Bookings 17

Legislative Essentials for Glamping Accommodation Lodgings Guide
Rob Farrow

- Distance Selling 18
    - Cancellations 18
    - Terms and Conditions 19
    - Card Charges 19
- Once You Are Open 21
    - Guest Registry 21
    - Luggage 21
    - Smoking In Public Places 23
    - Alcohol 23
    - Transportation of Guests 24
    - Furniture and Furnishings Fire 24
    - Childcare 25
- TV, Music & DVDs 27
    - Television 27
    - Music 27
    - DVDs 28
- Work Place Legislation 29
    - Employing Children 29
    - Working Hours 29
    - Migrant Workers 30
    - Data Protection 30
    - Electrical Items 31
    - Working at Height 32

Legislative Essentials for Glamping Accommodation Lodgings Guide
Rob Farrow

Safety Management 32

Product Safety – Gas Appliances 33

Product Safety – Electric & General 33

Work Equipment 35

Safe Manual Handling 36

Hazardous Substances 36

Legionnaire's disease 37

Legislative Essentials for Glamping Accommodation Lodgings Guide
Rob Farrow

Introduction

This guide has been written to provide an overview to those administering accommodation in the glamping industry. It is by no means exhaustive; however, it is our hope that the **Legislative Essentials for Glamping Accommodation Lodgings (LEGAL) Guide** will help increase awareness of some of the most important legislative requirements to those letting glamping accommodation. The aim of this guide is to provide an easy to digest overview of some of the most important legal requirements so that glamping accommodation owners can quickly become acquainted with their responsibilities - and not accidentally fall foul of the law.

For ease of reference the LEGAL Guide has been broken down into the steps you would follow when entering the glamping market; from permission to use land, to starting the actual glamping business and welcoming guests. This guide seeks to lay out the relevant legislation in chronological order.

This information guide is intended to assist in summarising and interpreting many—but not all—legislation and health and safety regulations which apply to UK glamping accommodation providers. This is merely the tip of the iceberg, designed to give a broad overview of the legislation required for the basic legal functioning of a small glamping site. We have not gone into detail for aspects such as play equipment, farm visits, animals, food preparation, activities provision etc. as these are not statutory to all sites. We recommend that if you remain in any doubt you seek out your own, independent legal advice.

The content is provided for general information only and must not be used for giving legal or other professional advice. If you require precise or detailed information on the legislation mentioned in this guide, or on the legal implications for you in particular, you should consult a professional legal adviser.

Whilst every care has been taken to ensure the accuracy of content, the author accepts no responsibility for loss (or consequential loss) occasioned to any person acting or refraining from action as a result of any statement made in this LEGAL guide.[1]

---

[1] **Disclaimer:** Whilst every effort has been made to ensure the accuracy of the information contained, we regret that we cannot be held responsible for any errors. This guide is not intended to be a definitive statement of the law in England. If you require precise or detailed information on the legislation mentioned in this guide, or on the legal implications for you in particular, you should consult a professional legal adviser.

Legislative Essentials for Glamping Accommodation Lodgings Guide
Rob Farrow

Foreword

Our industry has been embraced by people across the country and has grown rapidly as a result. There are now a plethora of glamping accommodation and variations available throughout England, many of these accommodations are provided by new entrants to the hospitality industry and/or are not located on traditional holiday parks. This provides a lovely experience for guests but a range of unique issues specific to accommodation providers.

The Glamping Association was originally founded over a decade ago and its purpose is to monitor the industry size and gather statistics. After a pod fire in the UK, the association saw that new entrants to the market needed more guidance to ensure that glamping accommodation was safe and that providers were not inadvertently breaking the law through lack of knowledge.

Today the Glamping Association is *the* Not For Profit Organisation representing glamping sites across the UK. Joining the Association is currently free and comes with a host of benefits including (but not limited to) a web listing and an enquiries service.

This book has been compiled not only to provide potential operators with an insight into what is required before you start, but also to arm existing operators with a brief oversight of the essentials required to meet their legal obligations. This book is based on the legislation current at the time of publication and only considers the law of England, different legislation may apply in other parts of the UK and **will** apply in other countries.

Legislative Essentials for Glamping Accommodation Lodgings Guide
Rob Farrow

If you require detailed information on any of the data or legislation given within this manuscript, we recommend seeking formal legal advice. For sites that wish to go further than the legal minimum shown in this book, The Association has partnered with leading independent accommodation assessors so members can display individual ratings. Please contact the association for more details.

We hope that this guide will prove insightful for glamping site operators both old and new.

Happy Glamping!

Rob Farrow
Author & Chairperson
Glamping Association
www.glampingassociation.co.uk

Before you start

"Over the years I've heard a lot of start-up stories from glamping sites. Some have been amusing, others funny. Most concerning were the ones that broke the law without even knowing it and had to suffer the consequences."

In 'Before you start' we look at some of the basic legislation that you need to meet before you can even begin to think about operating a glamping site. These aspects include various building regulations and other specifications that you must meet before you can commence trade. Without further ado, let's examine some of their finer points.

Planning

Unless you are utilising a 28 day policy or are an exempt organisation then it is highly likely that planning consent will be required to change the use of the area you wish to utilise for accommodation provision. If you are altering a building's function then you may need to apply for building regulations 'change of use' consent.

Suggested legislation to consult:

- Town and country planning act 1990
- Building regulations 2000
- Regulatory reform (fire safety) order 2005

Site Licence

Once you have attained planning permission you will then need to apply for a licence to operate. These tend to be either a camping or caravan site licence; or both a camping and caravan site licence if you are in possession of a mixture of tented and solid letting accommodation. Part of this will include fire safety.

Fire Safety

Almost all workplaces; including hotels, B&Bs and self-catering properties such as glamping accommodation, **must** have a designated and trained person responsible for fire safety on their premises (AKA a Fire Marshal / Fire Warden). In this process the 'responsible person' is required to adopt a self-assessment approach to fire safety in the workplace.

Suggested legislation to consult:

- Regulatory reform (fire safety) order 2005

Building Regulations

These apply if you erect, extend or materially alter a structure. They cover (but are not limited to); work and fittings such as structural alterations, drainage and sanitary installations, new heating installations, alterations that effect fire escape routes and electrical installations. If you build or change a structure for use as glamping accommodation or facilities for glamping, you should contact your local authority's building control department.

Suggested legislation to consult:

- Building Regulations 2000

Water

Guests must have access to an adequate supply of potable drinking water. If your water comes from a private water supply (groundwater source, private bore hole or well, spring stream or other surface water source) and is intended for human consumption (drinking, washing or food production) then the water must be tested by the local authority to ensure it is safe and free of contaminants.

Suggested legislation to consult:

- Food Safety Act, 1990
- Private Water Supplies Regulations (England) 2016

Rubbish

As a business with property that requires the payment of business rates, you are required to pay for a commercial waste collection service. This can either be through your council or a private firm.

Suggested legislation to consult:

- Controlled Waste Regulations 2012

Design

You must give people rights of access to your services, this applies to all holiday accommodation, even self-catering. You are required to make reasonable adjustments to your service in order to make it easier for a disabled guest to access and use. All business are required to accept service animals such as guide dogs.

Suggested legislation to consult:

- Equality Act, 2010

Signage

To erect outdoor signs and/or advertisements for your glamping site—such as at the entrance—a separate planning application will need to be submitted to your council. Advertising signs must not be misleading in any way.

Suggested legislation to consult:

- The Town and Country Planning (Control of Advertisements) Regulations, 2007
- Consumer Protection Regulations, 2008

First Aid

You must provide first aid facilities and equipment appropriate for your work place. At the very least you should have a person appointed to take charge of first aid, have a suitably stocked first-aid box and be familiar with local medical facilities.

Suggested legislation to consult:

- Management of Health and Safety at Work Regulations 1999

Insurance

Any glamping site will require specific and appropriate insurance in order to welcome paying guests and employ staff. There are various types available and you may need more than one variety of cover. Below, we attempt to summarise them for your benefit.

Employers Liability Insurance

As an employer, even if you just have someone cleaning your glamping accommodation or answering emails, you must have insurance to cover your employee's liability for any harm they may suffer at work. You must have employers' liability coverage for a minimum of £5m and you must display a copy of the insurance certificate at the place of business.

Suggested legislation to consult:

- Employers' Liability (Compulsory Insurance) Act, 1969

Public Liability Insurance

Although not a legal requirement PL is considered a necessity for businesses that interact with the public. PL insurance provides cover for your liability of any claim made against you from outside sources for injury, loss and damage. PL only covers claims against you by others, it does not cover loss or damage to your accommodation or property.

Suggested legislation to consult:

- Occupiers Liability Act, 1984

Appropriate and Adequate Insurance Cover

Whilst not a legal requirement; if you are receiving paying guests you should ensure you have appropriate and adequate insurance cover against theft or damage to guest property as well as for damage occurring as a result of business use of property in the accommodation. It is worth noting that household insurance policies will not cover the use of premises for business purposes.

Marketing

If you are advertising your accommodation your marketing statements must not be misleading or aggressive. If you compare your products to a rival's products you must comply to specific rules.

Suggested legislation to consult:

- Consumer Protection from Unfair Trading Regulations, 2008
- Business Protection from Misleading Marketing Regulations, 2008 (Business Protection Regulations) Comparison marketing.

Social Media

It is vital to understand that anything you post on a social media platform (such as Facebook, Twitter etc.) as a business falls under the Consumer Protection from Unfair Trading Regulations, 2008 and as such must meet the standards of the regulation.

Suggested legislation to consult:

- Consumer Protection from Unfair Trading Regulations, 2008

Bookings

One of the most complicated parts of welcoming guests is dealing with their enquiries and turning these into bookings. There are several regulations relating to the taking of bookings which cover services such as accommodation.

Taking Bookings

Businesses should set sliding scales of cancellation charges so they cover any likely losses incurred as a direct result from the cancellation.

Suggested legislation to consult:

- Trading Standards office

Honouring Bookings

When a guest makes a booking you have entered into a contract with them. Once a booking has been made you cannot then cancel on the guest without breaking that contract.

Suggested legislation to consult:

- Trading Standards office

Distance Selling

Regulations apply to goods and services that are not purchased in a 'face-to-face' transaction; such as that sold via the internet or by phone. This exists because the customer has not been able to inspect the goods or service prior to purchase.

The information that must be provided for these transactions includes the business name, the goods or services being sold, payment and delivery arrangements, and the consumers' right to cancel their orders.

Suggested legislation to consult:

- Consumer Contracts (Information, Cancellation and Additional Charges) Regulations, 2013

Cancellations

It is recommended that you have a cancellation policy in place. This must be made clear to guests before they book, when guests should confirm they understand and accept your cancellation policy. It should also be easily available to read on your website. Your cancellation policy's terms and conditions must be fair to the guest. Normally sites charge a cancellation fee or a cancellation forfeits any deposit.

If you accept a booking and then cancel the guests booking you are in breach of the booking contract. You must find the guest alternative accommodation to the same standard or better.

Suggested sources to consult:

- Trading Standards

Terms and Conditions

If you need to comply with the Package Travel Regulations you will need to have booking terms and conditions. However, even if you do not need to comply with the package Travel Regulation it is strongly recommended you have terms and conditions that cover deposits and cancellations at the very least. Terms and conditions should be provided to guests before they book.

Regardless of anything you have in place the law requires you to provide your service with reasonable skill and care. You cannot use terms and conditions to exclude yourself from your legal obligations such as ensuring a safe environment under the health and safety act. Legally speaking, terms and conditions cannot be used to limit your liability to a guest due to death or injury through your negligence.

Suggested sources to consult:

- Competition and Markets Authority; Guide on Unfair Contract Terms

Card Charges

It is unlawful to charge additional fees when a customer uses a credit or debit card, or other payment systems like PayPal, to make a purchase.

Legislative **E**ssentials for **G**lamping **A**ccommodation Lodgings Guide
Rob Farrow

Suggested legislation to consult:

- EU Second Payment Services Directive (PSD2)

Once You Are Open

Once you open your site and welcome guests further legislation applies to your guests, their records, their property, your staff, entertainment, music, alcohol, furniture and furnishings – some of which we have outlined below.

Guest Registry

A record of the name and nationality of all guests over the age of 16 must be kept. This must include their full name and nationality. For non-British, Irish or Commonwealth guests you must also record their passport number and place of issue or other nationality / Identity documents as well as their next destination.

Suggested legislation to consult:

- Immigration (Hotel Records) Order, 1972

Luggage

If you accept guests overnight, the law requires that you take responsibility for the safekeeping of all reasonable items of luggage the guest brings. This means you are liable in the event of loss or damage. You may be fully liable if the loss or damage is due to negligence or a wilful act by you or your staff, if the items had been entrusted to you for safekeeping or if you have refused to accept them for safekeeping.

Legislative Essentials for Glamping Accommodation Lodgings Guide
Rob Farrow

You may limit your liability by displaying this statutory notice prominently i.e. at reception or the main entrance:

SCHEDULE NOTICE
LOSS OF OR DAMAGE TO GUESTS' PROPERTY

Under the Hotel Proprietors Act 1956, a hotel proprietor may in certain circumstances be liable to make good any loss of or damage to a guest's property even though it was not due to any fault of the proprietor or staff of the hotel.

This liability however—

(a) extends only to the property of guests who have engaged sleeping accommodation at the hotel;

(b) is limited to £50 for any one article and a total of £100 in the case of any one guest, except in the case of property which has been deposited, or offered for deposit, for safe custody;

(c) does not cover motor-cars or other vehicles of any kind or any property left in them, or horses or other live animals.

This notice does not constitute an admission either that the Act applies to this hotel or that liability thereunder attaches to the proprietor of this hotel in any particular case.

A different notice exists for London.

Suggested legislation to consult:

- Hotel Proprietors Act, 1956

Smoking In Public Places

In England Smoking has been banned in all enclosed spaces and places of work since 1 July 2007. As such, you are required to display legible no-smoking signage that can be seen by both customers and staff.

Suggested legislation to consult:
- Health Act, 2006

Alcohol

This applies even if you include "free" alcoholic drinks such as a welcome bottle of wine in the accommodation. As you are providing accommodations for a charge; the law sees it that you will have covered the cost of the alcohol in your price and are therefore considered to be selling alcohol. To sell alcohol you must have a licensed premises and a designated premises supervisor who has taken the appropriate exams and holds a personal licence.

Suggested legislation to consult:
- Licensing Act, 2003

Transportation of Guests

Anyone providing a frequent service of transport for guests; be it to and from a station, coach, ferry or airport, local town or pub etc. (or in a vehicle with more than 16 seats) will require one of two Passenger Service Vehicle (PSV) licences.

For the provision of an on-demand transport service which transports them wherever they wish to go you will require a taxi or private hire licence. This requires a criminal record check, a test of your local road and destination knowledge, a medical exam and specialist insurance.

Anyone transporting guests, even on a rare basis and without charge must have appropriate business insurance for the business activity of transporting people and carry out a health and safety check.

Suggested legislation to consult:

- Passenger Service Vehicle (PSV) licence
- Criminal Records Bureau

Furniture and Furnishings Fire

All furniture and furnishing (new and second hand) must meet relevant fire resistance standards to comply with a safety test.

These include (but are not limited to):

- Upholstered furniture must pass a cigarette resistance test.
- Cover fabric (loose and or permanent) will have a match resistance test.

- Filling and stuffing material for all furniture must pass ignitability tests.
- All new upholstered furniture and covers must have a permanent label showing compliance with fire safety requirements. (This excludes mattresses and bedding).

These regulations would feasibly apply to aspects in glamping accommodation such as yurt wall linings or silks.

For second-hand furniture the regulation only applies to furniture made after 1950, unless they are being significantly altered or reupholstered. When reupholstering furniture you must use compliant materials.

Fire inhibiting sprays are not advise due to durability issues. The Local Government Association advise extreme caution in the consideration of using fire inhibiting sprays.

Suggested legislation to consult:
- Furniture and Furnishing (Fire) (Safety) Regulations, 1988

Childcare

Accommodation providers that offer a childcare service or children's activity for children under the age of eight for more than 2 hours are required to register with Ofsted. This applies regardless of whether the child belongs to a member of staff or a guest.

TV, Music & DVDs

Television

If you provide a device that TV programmes can be viewed on, you must apply for a hotel licence (TV and Mobile Units Television Licence. This applies whether programmes are viewed on a TV, computer, DVD recorder, mobile phone, digital box, games console or other device. Guests are not covered by their home licence.

Suggested legislation to consult:

- Copyright, Design and Patents Act 1988

Music

If you play music in public (in guest rooms /accommodation, reception or public spaces on your site) or provide a radio, TV etc. you will need to pay a licence to the Performing Rights Society (PRS) for Music. The PRS only relates to the music and you will also need to pay a separate licence related to the recording, regardless of whether you are playing a record, tape, CD or digital download. This is issued by Phonographic Performance Limited.

Suggested legislation to consult:

- Copyright, Design and Patents Act 1988

DVDs

If you offer films to your guests you need a licence from the relevant film studio or licensing body. DVDs can then be played on a variety of devices. You do not need a licence if guests bring their own DVDs.

Suggested legislation to consult:

- Copyright, Design and Patents Act 1988

Work Place Legislation

If you have anyone working for you then work place legislation will apply to your glamping site.

Employing Children

It is illegal to employ anyone under the age of 13. Children between 13 – 16 can only be employed part time; note there are considerable restrictions. Children can only undertake full-time employment once they reach the minimum school leaving age of 16. Under 18's can only be in full time employment if they are on an apprenticeship or traineeship scheme. Unless the Child is a family member, you must undertake a separate Health and Safety Assessment of their position that takes into consideration their age and lack of experience.

Suggested legislation to consult:

- Children (protection at Work) Regulations 2000
- Childcare Facilities and the Children Act, 1989

Working Hours

Applies to all accommodation providers that have employees. Employers must take steps to ensure that employees do not work more than an average of 48 hours a week excluding lunch breaks. Employees can choose to work longer by signing a Working Time Regulations Opt-Out Agreement. Employees are entitled to 5.6 weeks paid leave a year.

Suggested legislation to consult:

- The Working Time Regulations, 1998

Migrant Workers

Employers must ensure that staff and prospective staff from outside the UK have permission to work in the UK. A foreign national must provide an employer with necessary documentation. You are required to check any documentation provided to ensure that the potential employee is entitled to work in the UK and that their documents are genuine.

Suggested legislation to consult:

- UK Borders Act, 2007
- Public Register of Authentic Identification and Travel Documents Online (PRADO)

Data Protection

Holding or using personal information on individuals (guests or employees) is regulated. The three essential requirements are to:

1. Notify the Information Commissioner.

2. Follow data protection principles.
3. Comply with the rights of data subjects.

If you only hold personal data on a manual filling system you do not need to notify the Information Commissioner.

NOTE: from 25 May 2018 and irrespective of the UK leaving the EU; a new piece of legislation known as GDPR applies. GDPR broadens the definition of personal data to include 'personal identifiers' such as IP addresses. It is safe to assume that information covered by previous data protection legislation will also fall within GDPR.

Suggested legislation to consult:

- Data Protection Act 1998
- General Data Protection Regulation 2018

Electrical Items

You are required to ensure that all electrical equipment supplied is safe. 'Safe' means there is no risk of death, injury or damage from the electrical equipment. New items should carry a CE marking when purchased.

Suggested legislation to consult:

- Electrical Equipment (Safety) Regulations, 2016

Working at Height

Employers are required to avoid having staff work at height where possible. Where it is unavoidable employers must take measures to ensure that the person working at height does not fall. There must be a risk assessment carried out before an employee works at a height. People involved in working at a height must be competent and adequately trained and supervised. Working at height means where a person can fall and could be injured, there is no minimum height. This includes working at ground level above openings such as an open man hole, drain cover or cellar opening.

Suggested legislation to consult:

- Work at Height Regulations, 2005

Safety Management

To avoid accidents and ill health employers must manage health and safety at work. Employers are required to carry out a risk assessment of the health and safety risks to employees at work and any other people arising from work activities which is 'suitable and sufficient'.

Suggested legislation to consult:

- Management of Health and Safety at Work Regulations, 1999

Product Safety – Gas Appliances

You must ensure gas appliances are safely maintained and in good condition. You are required to have an annual safety check from a Gas Safe registered engineer and keep a record of the inspection for 2 years.

Suggested legislation to consult:

- Gas Safety (Installation and Use) Regulations 1998.

Product Safety – Electric & General

Both new and second hand electrical equipment supplied must be in a safe condition. All products supplied for consumers to use, such as kettles, hair-dryer in accommodation or other utensils for guests, should be safe. You should ensure that you only supply safe products for guests and ensure the product remains safe throughout the period of use.

Suggested legislation to consult:

- Electrical Equipment (Safety) Regulations 2016
- General product safety regulations, 2005

Gas and Log Burner Safety

Every year there are fatalities from carbon monoxide poisoning caused by poorly installed or badly maintained gas appliances and flues. You must ensure gas fittings and log burner flues are in safe condition, that an annual safety check is carried out for each gas appliance by a Gas Safe registered engineer and log burners by an approved engineer and keep a written record of the inspection for a minimum of two years.

Stoves and log burners should have a flame retardant mat around them and use a spark arrester on the top of the flue. Combustible items must be kept away from the stove and a fire extinguisher should be kept close by. You should have signage to ensure guests do not touch a hot stove surface.

To avoid Carbon Monoxide Poisoning guests must be told to take precautions such as (but not limited to):

1. When using a tent stove tent must be well ventilated.
2. Extinguish stoves before going to bed.

Suggested legislation to consult:

- The Smoke and Carbon Monoxide Alarm (England) Regulations 2015

Health and Safety at Work

The Health and Safety at Work Act (HSWA) places responsibilities and the general duties of health and safety on all people at work, including employers, employees and the self-employed. Employers are responsible for ensuring, so far as is reasonably practicable, the health, safety and welfare of all your employees at work.

Employers / site operators also have a wider responsibility to anyone else who could be affected by your work activities, e.g., guests /visitors, casual workers or contractors.

In addition, the person who controls the site (known as the 'occupier') is liable for the safety of everyone who comes onto the glamping site or 'premises'.

Suggested legislation to consult:

- Health and Safety at Work Act 1974
- Occupiers Liability Act 1957 & 1984

Work Equipment

The equipment provided for work must be suitable for the job, properly installed, properly maintained, in good repair and safe to operate. Training must also be given and instructions and the suppliers or manufacturer's instructions must be followed.

Equipment must conform to EC product safety directives. This is not restricted to just your own staff and also applies to employees that bring their own equipment and the self-employed you contract to work for you (such as a cleaner that comes in to clean accommodation).

Suggested legislation to consult:

- Provision and Use of Work Equipment Regulations, 1998

Safe Manual Handling

As an employer you are required to assess the risk of tasks and take appropriate precautions. You must ensure employees are not required to undertake any manual handling operations at work if there is a risk of them being injured. For employers who require employees to carry out manual handling the risks must be properly assessed and minimised as far as is reasonably practicable.

Suggested legislation to consult:

- Management of Health and Safety at Work Regulations, 1999
- Manual Handling Operations Regulations, 1992

Hazardous Substances

As an employer you have a duty to remove employees' exposure to hazardous substances, or to adequately control it. You must assess all hazardous substances. Hazardous substances will normally be identifiable from the label. Products used for general cleaning, pest control, drain cleaning, gardening and other chemical products used in cleaning or maintaining accommodation, cooking facilities, bathrooms or grounds can also be hazardous. To assist in your assessment you might need a products Safety Data Sheet which lists products contents and the related dangers; you can then plan how to best prevent harm and control the substance.

Suggested legislation to consult:

- Control of Substances Hazardous to Health Regulations, 2002 (COSHH)

Legionnaire's disease

Legionnaire's disease is a potentially fatal bacterium that can cause a significant health risk and is classed as a hazardous substance. Legionnaire's conditions can occur where water stays between 20 – 45 degrees C, such as water tanks, spas, hot tubs, air conditioning units and showers are most common breeding grounds for legionnaire's disease.

If you are a seasonal site or have periods where the water system is not in regular use, take precautions to ensure water does not stagnate. If vacant for long periods you should drain or flush the system before guests arrive.

And Finally...

I hope this introductory guide helps assist sites in providing safe and legal accommodation. It is by no means and exhaustive list and I cannot stress enough that if you have any questions you should seek professional legal advice. However, I hope that it will allow operators of glamping sites a sufficient overview to avoid common pitfalls. Coming from a family that have operated holiday parks and provided accommodation for over half a century; I have learnt that one imperative is overarching in this industry and it is no coincidence it is the motto of the scout movement. For happy, safe glamping we must be ever vigilant and Be Prepared.

Printed in Great Britain
by Amazon